At the Library

Illustrations

Penny Dann

Picture Credits

© Charles Gupton/Tony Stone Images: cover
© David Young Wolff/Tony Stone Images: 8
© Frank Siteman/Tony Stone Images: 3, 6, 20
© Gregg Andersen/Gallery 19: 10, 14, 22, 24, 28
© Jack McConnell: 4, 16, 18
© Jim Pickerell/Tony Stone Images: 30
© Kindra Clineff/Tony Stone Images: 12
© Robert E. Daemmrich/Tony Stone Worldwide: 26

Library of Congress Cataloging-in-Publication Data

Greene, Carol.

At the library / by Carol Greene.
p.   cm.
Summary: Simple text introduces the activities,
users, employees, and contents of a public library.
ISBN 1-56766-562-4 (library reinforced : alk. paper)
1. Libraries—Juvenile literature.
[1. Libraries.]   I. Title.

Z665.5.G74   1998   98-3484
027—dc21   CIP
                    AC

At the Library

By Carol Greene

The Child's World®, Inc.

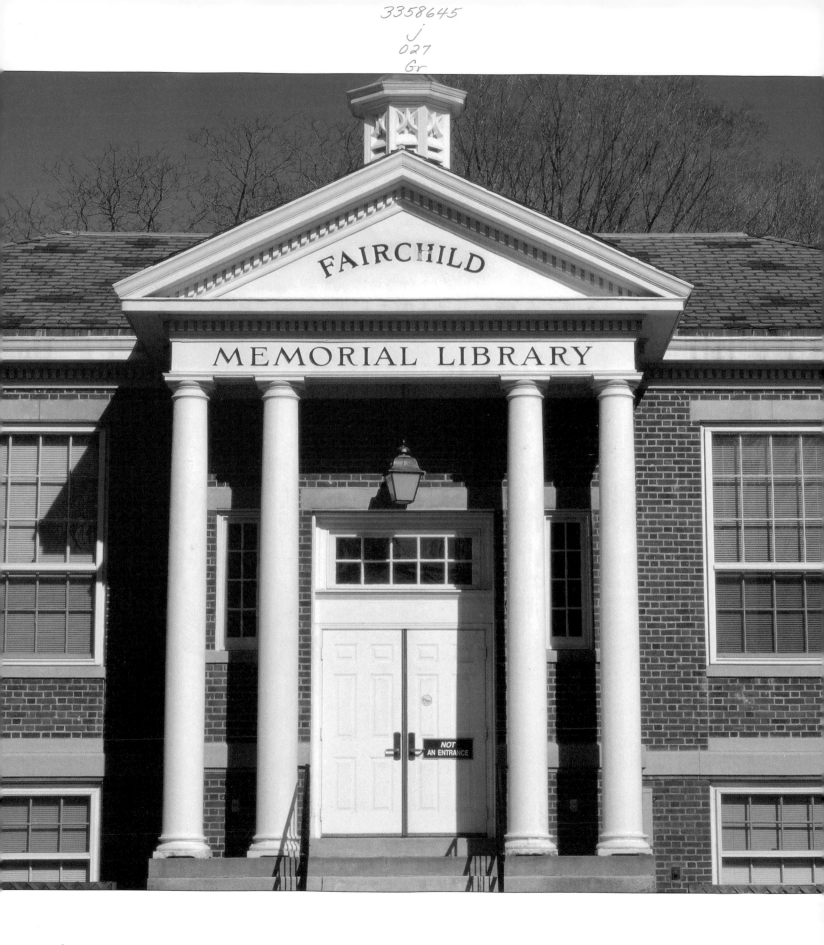

FAIRCHILD

MEMORIAL LIBRARY

NOT
AN ENTRANCE

4

TOOT! TOOT! VROOM!

This library is on a busy street. There are many kinds of noises to hear.

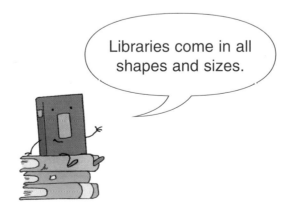

Libraries come in all shapes and sizes.

RUSTLE! SHUFFLE!

But the noises inside the library are quiet noises. People look and read and write and think.

When you talk in the library, be sure to talk quietly.

CLICK! CLICK! TAP!

These people are looking for information. The library's computers help them find it.

Computers make libraries easier to use. They have information about thousands of books.

FLIP! FLAP!

This boy is reading a sports magazine. The library keeps magazines on shelves. These shelves are called **stacks**.

THUD!

This girl is learning about bugs. She is using a big book in the **reference room**.

Books from the reference room must stay in the library.

CLICK!

This lady is reading a story from an old newspaper. Newspapers are often put in tiny pictures called **microfilm**. That way, they take up less room on the shelves.

HMMMM!

Finding just the right book can be hard sometimes. To help, books about the same things are kept in the same place.

Libraries must be very orderly so people can find things easily.

"Once upon a time. . ."

These children are listening to a story. The children's room is a special part of the library. It has lots of chairs and interesting books to read.

DA-DA-DEE-DUM!

Many libraries have places where you can listen to music on **headphones**. You can also listen to books while you look at the pictures.

Headphones let people listen to things without bothering others.

CLICK! TAP! RUSTLE!

In this area, the librarians are busy. They are ordering new books and tapes. They use computers to keep track of what they are doing.

FLIP! FLIP!

Here librarians get the books ready for people to use. They make sure the books are what they ordered. Then they put information about the books into the computer.

Some libraries put a special strip in each book. If someone tries to steal the book, the strip sets off an alarm.

At the main desk, people check out books. The librarian uses a computer to mark down which books the people are taking home.

The books are rubbed on a machine. Then the special strip won't set off the alarm.

THUMP!

People return books here.

JINGLE! JINGLE!

If the books are late, the people must pay a **fine**.

It is very important to return your books on time.

George had a sweet tooth.

He just couldn't stop himself from eating sweets.

"You know what they say about too much sugar," said Martha.

"Let's not discuss it," said George.

GOODBYE!

Now it is time to take your library books home. Make sure you know when to return them. See you soon!

GLOSSARY

computers (kom–PYOO–terz)
Computers are special machines that hold information. They also give answers quickly.

fine (FINE)
A fine is money people must pay if they return library books late.

headphones (HED FOHNZ)
Headphones are little speakers that fit over your ears. When you listen to things on headphones, you are the only person who can hear what is playing.

microfilm (MY–kro–film)
Microfilm holds tiny pictures of magazines and newspapers.

reference room (REH–fer–ens ROOM)
The reference room has special books that hold lots of information. These books must always stay in the library.

stacks (STAKS)
Stacks are shelves where libraries keep magazines and books.

INDEX

CAROLE GREENE has published over 200 books for children. She also likes to read books, make teddy bears, work in her garden, and sing. Ms. Greene lives in Webster Groves, Missouri.